SIMPLE TIMES

**FREE RIVER PRESS
FOLK LITERATURE SERIES**

Robert Wolf, General Editor

SIMPLE TIMES

by

Clara Leppert

FREE RIVER PRESS

ISBN# 1-878781-07-3
by Free River Press
All rights reserved

Free River Press
RR 2, Box 96
Lansing, IA 52151

In memory
of
Clarence,
Roger and Howard,
and to
Bob and Ruth,
to my grandchildren,
and great-grandchildren

FOREWORD

Writing that transmits culture passes on information, technical or otherwise. In the Middle Ages this information was frequently transmitted under the guise of a good story, but nowadays we often find a split between entertainment and information. There is seldom that split for folk writers, who are concerned with passing on the stuff of their lives: local history, customs, thoughts, daily relations. And they do so in a matter-of-fact way. Their writing is of a piece with their lives.

Clara Leppert's writing is a reflection of Clara, and exemplifies the best qualities of good folk writing: it is direct, plain, and unpretentious. When she read one of her pieces for a National Public Radio story, people called from across the country, wanting to know how they could get the book that contained the story, "Wolves."

Clara's voice, its intonation and wonderful quavering sweetness, itself evokes qualities of long ago. No wonder, for Clara--unworldly, living and growing up in a corner of northeastern Iowa--has in effect remained untouched by the corruption of a world increasingly urbanized, increasingly mechanized, increasingly depersonalized.

Only after living in northeastern Iowa for one year could I begin to understand how rootedness in place, without heavy dependence on rapid transportation, provided the nurturing for community. The rootedness of small towns and rural populations in the last century was what gave many American communities their distinct qualities. For the farm families, who usually traveled to town no more than once a week, this engendered an unworldliness, a self-reliance, and, at the same time, an understanding of the need for community.

When the present crop of farmers passes away, with them will go their way of life and their simplicity, directness, and honesty. For the urban dweller, so often armored with cynicism, this seems quaint, unbelievable, hardly enviable. But the problem is that once these farmers go, we have only written records to show us how people once behaved in community. And the cynics are likely to deny that such community ever existed, thus making it ever more difficult to recapture.

But Clara's book, I believe, will remain as a record of what rural life was once like, and a reminder of how it might be rebuilt. Not so much with technical know-how as with benevolence and the qualities which make a man or woman a full human being. It has been a delight knowing this wonderful eighty-four-year-old neighbor.

Simple Times was developed in a Free River Press writing workshop, which was denied funding by the Iowa Humanities Board. It is ironic that the same board spends money to send a woman around Iowa to talk about her ten-month stay in Yugoslavia, and supports a professor's lectures on Central and South America.

> **ROBERT WOLF**
> **Good Friday, 1993**
> **Lansing, Iowa**

Thanks to Steven Meinbresse and Cherry Smith
for their continued support.
Cover photo and decorations by Bonnie Koloc

Prologue

I was born May 3, 1909. As I grew up, I loved to climb trees. I would sit on a branch close to the top and not hold on to anything. It would scare my younger sisters.

I loved to ride horses. I wanted them to be spirited so they would be speedy.

I liked the peppy popular music.

It was fun to go to my dad's woods, watch the creek as it rippled, and listen as it sang a song. We picked May flowers, violets, blood root, and Dutchman Breeches.

Now, I am older. I don't even care to climb a ladder, and would be scared to get on a horse.

I love soft music, especially waltzes.

It is a joy to send cards to relatives and friends who have a special day.

I love to go to church and sing and pray with the others. If I am awake at night I pray. Someone said, "If you can't sleep at night, don't count sheep, talk to the Shepherd."

I Am Clara

I am Clara, the middle daughter. I was born on a sunny, warm spring day, May 3, 1909 at the home of my parents, Adolph Siekmeier and Carolena (Lena) Nagel. Uncle Jake Siekmeier wrote in the *North Fork*, a local paper, "After a long, dreary, cold winter, baby Siekmeier brings spring." My older sisters are Mary, Anna, and Lydia, the younger are Esther, Ruth, and Dorothy.

Mother said Dad wanted me to be named Clara, because it was a good Danish name, but he couldn't say it very well. He called me Clarie. My younger sisters called me La La or

Da Da.

I am glad to have grown up in a family where we were taught to love the Lord and to go to Sunday school and church. One of the first things I remember from my childhood is family devotions. After we ate breakfast, Dad read a chapter out of the Bible, and we all knelt by our chairs while he prayed. Again in the evening, before we went to bed, he read another chapter from the Bible.

We usually wore white dresses to church. We put large bows in our braided hair and wore hats and gloves. It was very important to have a new hat and dress for Easter and new clothes for Christmas services. Our skirts had lace and tucks and were starched. Unless our dresses were plenty heavy, we had to wear two skirts. Even though we usually had braids, our hair would get tangled, and we would yell when our older sisters combed our hair.

Mother usually shaved Dad Sunday mornings. If he got shaved in town she would reprimand him saying, "Why did you get shaved in town? You know I would have shaved you." If he didn't get shaved in town, she'd ask, "Why didn't you get shaved in town? Now I have to shave you."

We drove to church with horses and buggy or sled. Dad had quincy quite a lot in the winter time. He finally had to have his tonsils out. If he couldn't go to church, Mother would drive. Some of the winters we had a lot of snow. For two miles we would have to go up high banks or in people's fields, and sometimes the sled would tip over. We'd have to pick up the straw and blankets and get back in. When the next two miles were graveled, the snow scraping off the sled made a gritty noise, but it didn't seem hard for the horses to pull. They were always well fed and well taken care of.

When we got to church we had to tie the horses in the hitching yard and put blankets on them to keep them from getting chilled. Every Sunday, Mrs. Sherman would brush a little dust or horse hair from Mother's dark coat. The two families were always very good friends.

Years later, in 1918, Dad bought a one-passenger Buick. It had two jump seats. We had a really full load sometimes, but it would still move in mud up to the hubcaps. We'd have to get on our knees to put on the chains and hang side curtains. Side curtains fit on the side windows where modern cars have glass. On our way to church Dad would say, "Don't drive quite so fast," and Mother would say, "Drive a little faster or we're going to be late."

Farming a Long Time Ago

As I was growing up, farming was a family affair. Each person had a job. Dad always fed the pigs, but the women took care of the chickens and got the cows from the pasture. Dad planted the corn and sowed the oats. All of the farm work was done with horses. We girls helped with putting up hay, shocking grain, and husking corn. Mother would see to it that the younger ones brought us lunch. When each of us girls was about eight, we were old enough to milk a cow.

Mother took care of the big gas engine that turned the separator. I don't know how many times she fixed it. The milk was given to the pigs, and the cream hauler came for the cream that had been put in ten gallon cans. The hauler put these cans in his truck.

In the fall when the grain was ripe we girls shocked the grain, putting six bundles together, and one on top to keep the rain off. Barley bundles scratched our arms and made us itch. Later when the corn was ripe, we would husk it, two rows at a time. The horses would follow the rows and stop and go as we told them.

Putting up hay was a big job. Mother mowed the hay, and also ran the side deliver, a machine that put the hay in windrows. When the hay was dry, one of us girls would drive the horses on the hay rack, pulling the hay loader, which was a tall machine with rollers that rolled the hay onto the rack. Dad would distribute the hay evenly on the rack.

When we unloaded the hay, mother stuck the fork, which had two sharp prongs, into the hay. Then she'd push a lever that would hold the hay. The hay fork had a rope on it and at the other end of the barn you had two horses that would pull the fork and hay up high into the barn.

One of us girls would drive the team to the other side of the barn, pulling up the hay fork. Dad would yell "whoa" when the fork of hay was where he wanted it in the hay mow (the storage area), and mother would trip the fork. One time she didn't think and tied the rope to the hay rack. It raised quite high in the air before the horses could be stopped.

We had about three hundred chickens each year. It was a lot of work with the hens, who sometimes wouldn't set on their fifteen eggs, and we would cover the eggs with a box for awhile. We had to catch the hens, who sometimes pecked us, and put them in their little houses, then catch the fluffy little chickens when it rained. Mother had an incubator, and we turned all the eggs twice a day, I think, but it seemed that so many eggs didn't hatch.

We were all glad to do what we could to help. We loved each other and our faithful horses, and we loved our life on the farm.

Childhood Games

We liked to play horse, especially after a rain, as it was fun splashing in the mud. I was usually the horse driven by my younger sisters. We stuffed our dresses in our panties and Dad would say, "You are my little pants boys." I liked to hear him say that. I ate gooseberries, pretending it was oats. They were awfully sour, but it was fun, being that it bothered my sisters' ears.

We loved to walk to the woods. Mary had cleaned leaves away from a damp spot on the bluff. There was a little spring, we always called it "Mary's Little Spring." Sometimes we found pretty berries on the weeds to make our mud pies pretty. Dad never told anyone where an Indian grave was, he was afraid someone would dig it up, but we always looked for it.

We girls played a lot in the attic with our dolls, there were steps from the bathroom into the attic. We tenderly cared for our dolls and sewed for them, but their heads were so porcelain and so breakable. They were beautiful and had eyes that would go to sleep.

I Wasn't Always Good

I wasn't always good. I don't know if anyone knew I teased the huge turkey gobbler. I would stand on the safe side of the lawn fence, point my finger at him and say, "Gobble, gobble, gobble." He would get very angry and got so he would fly at us when we went in the big yard. Mother finally decided he had better be put in the big roasting pan.

I also teased Lydia's little terrier dog, pointing at her and saying, "Bow wow." One day I didn't get my left forefinger back in time and she took a piece of flesh out of it. I still have the scar.

One day I was asked to take the hammer back to the separator house. I thought, instead of carrying it there, it would be much more fun to drive by in the little wagon and throw it in. I had good speed on the little wagon and threw in the hammer as I had planned, but I didn't know anyone was in the building. I hit Anna smack on the head. She didn't scold me much, but she had a big lump on her head, of course, and I felt real sorry, but being sorry didn't help the lump.

One day Uncle Fred and Aunt Mary left their Ford car in Dad's machine shed, while they went away for a couple of days with Mother and Dad. Lydia and I didn't know how to run a car, but thought it would be great fun to try. One of us steered and the other gave a push and suddenly the Ford was down in the yard. We didn't know how to get the car started, but kept trying until we had it humming and sputtering and safely back in the shed again.

Family

We girls didn't do much quarrelling. It didn't pay to get Mother "riled up" and "after us", and if Dad heard us not talking very nice to each other he'd say, "Girls, don't rouse one another's tempers." I was too little to remember when he had a bad temper, but I remember Mother's temper very well. She spanked or whipped me many times. Sometimes I knew I had been naughty. Other times I didn't know what I had done wrong. One time I was standing by the range and she suddenly kept hitting me with a nice big pancake turner until it broke it two. I didn't feel sorry about the pancake turner, but my rear didn't feel so good for a long time. I never knew why I was whipped.

I was almost ten when Dorothy was born, but didn't know Mother was expecting a baby. Mother didn't seem well and didn't have loving patience with the new baby. Many evenings I walked around and around the house with Dorothy to get her to sleep. I liked to do it.

We weren't a huggy, kissy family, but we knew our parents loved us. I never remember sitting on either Dad or Mother's lap, but it was only once I saw Dad spank any of us.

Dad

Dad said, "Be thankful to have both jam and butter on your bread, many folks would be glad to have just bread." It got on his nerves when we "scratched" butter on our crackers, as he called it. He also didn't like it when we cut the bread thin. He had trouble with pronunciation, as I do yet. After learning the Danish language, and the German and English languages after coming to this country, some words were hard for him to say. He would tell us, "You cut the bread so tin, tin as a piece of paper," so we would try to do better the next time.

Dad loved bananas, they didn't have them in Denmark. When his family came to this country and were in Chicago on the way here, he was eating the whole banana when someone told him to take the peel off. He often bought bananas when he went to town, also chocolate stars and what he called little chocolate hills.

He didn't always go with us places, he visited people and talked about religion. He had a great knowledge of the Bible. Landsgards and others said they asked him to talk about the Bible to them. Landsgards, being Norwegian, could understand his Dane.

During his prime years, Dad was very strong. I was told he could bend a horseshoe straight, lift a barrel of salt, also lift the end of a threshing machine. At one time he carried a mule who wouldn't drink to the tank.

He said when he couldn't sleep, he was on his knees praying that all of us would go to Heaven.

We Loved Aunt Mary and Uncle Fred

We all loved Aunt Mary and Uncle Fred and were always glad when they came to see us. Aunt Mary was Mother's sister and Uncle Fred was Dad's brother. They didn't have any children, so they gave us much affection. I sat by Aunt Mary, knowing she would soon open up her purse and give me a cough drop. It took the place of candy. They were delicious. She would tell the story about "The Goat and the Seven Little Kids." I thought it was a terrible ghost story, but the next time she came, I would ask her to tell it again. One night when Aunt Mary stayed over she came to Mother's room in the middle of the night where us younger ones slept, knelt by Mother's bed and said, "Lena, my heart, my heart. I'm dying." It surely scared me, but Mother got out of bed and gave her something to comfort her. She seemed all right the next day.

When Aunt Mary and Uncle Fred came to see us they would leave as soon as they had eaten dinner because Uncle Fred was afraid a storm would come up. One day Dad said, "Can't you stay a little longer? There isn't a cloud in the sky." The sky was as beautiful clear and blue as a jewel. Uncle Fred said, "No, the wind might blow up a storm and it might rain." Aunt Mary and Uncle Fred never had a lot of money, but she bought each of my sisters and me a ring for our confirmations. Mine is a yellow sapphire. It will always be very special.

The McCabe's

I helped out at five or six places. It was a very hard thing for me to do, but the folks felt it was the only Christian thing to do. I helped Cora McCabe with cleaning and at threshing. It wasn't easy to keep an even temperature with the ranges, sometimes the pie burned, but she would calmly say, "Just snag off a little bit of the black." Wages weren't big, but I was proud walking home with a quarter in my pocket.

We and the McCabes were always very good friends. We went to the Catholic church for their children's first communion and confirmation. As we went up the steps, the friendly people would say, "You can sit in our pew." It seems to me there must have been fifty or sixty young children receiving their first communion. The girls were all dressed with white veils and dresses.

Peddlers

We had a peddler who came every month or two for years. He came in the evening so he could stay overnight. We had to wait until morning to see what he had in his big leather-like bag. He always gave mother coffee beans to grind to prove he had good coffee. He had dress fabric and a lot of things. He gave us kids little trinkets.

We all felt bad when Lydia had blood poisoning in her arm. A man came selling Watkins or something (they drove horses yet), and he wanted to prove his salve was good. We put salve on a sore on her arm, and we felt that caused the poisoning. Dr. Huecker came every day for fourteen days, and lanced it in five places. She had a lot of pain. When she would cry we were told to go down the lane a ways. Her arm was very stiff. Mother had a little outfit with rubber wheels, she colled her arm every night. Her arm never got so she could bend it like her right arm. We were glad she got along as well as she did.

Christmas

Christmas was always a big event. We looked forward to the Christmas Eve program at church, to our sacks of nuts and, maybe, to an apple and orange. Those who could, paid for the sacks. We would get a gift from our Sunday school teacher. It was good to hear the people sing, "Der Christbaum ist der Schonste Baum" as the candles were lit. In English it was "The Christmas tree is the fairest tree." Candles were in little metal holders. Men stood with a wet mop to put a little fire out if it started.

The program was very special. Dad didn't go, but he would stay up to put the horses in the barn. Mother drove the horses' sled. There were probably deep snow drifts for two miles. We had to go on the banks of the road and through some fields, and then for two miles on gravel. The sled runners made lots of noise and we felt sorry for the horses. When we got to town, people were driving around the streets, the bells on the horses' harness making such beautiful Christmas music.

Town

I often drove Nellie or Daisy, our horses, to help drive cattle to town to sell. These were war times. We didn't have much white flour. We could only buy fifty pounds worth of sugar at a time. After we got to town Dad gave each of us a dollar. We decided right away to get fifty cents worth of sugar each to help out on Mother's baking. We still had fifty cents left. It said on the window of the Red Geranium cafe: banana splits fifty cents. We walked by many times looking at the pretty picture of the banana split. It looked so good, and we had never had one, but fifty cents was a lot of money. We finally decided to spend it and slowly ate our banana split. Beside the banana there were three kinds of ice cream and lots of syrup and a red cherry on each dip of ice cream. We always remember that special event.

One day Ruth and I went to town to take food to Esther, who was rooming there. We had the cutter which tipped easily. Unexpectedly, the cutter runners followed the railroad track instead of crossing it and tipped over and the horses ran away. We had to stop when one was on each side of a telephone pole. Daisy was hurt quite badly and was never quite as good any more. Dad felt awfully bad. I did too. He said, "It's too late for this time, watch out for the next."

One day we had a phone call. The horse we had loaned Uncle Fred was in town, and he was through with her. I was to get her, tying her behind the buggy. She looked pretty old and feeble, but I tied her behind the buggy and started for home. I went on the road past Aunt Ida's and Uncle Herman's to avoid going past the train. Uncle Herman was on the porch. He said, "You'll never get that horse home alive Clara," but I did. It was a slow trip. The horses walked all the way, but I did get home all right.

School and Town

I was a freshman when Anna and Lydia were seniors. For the first time I didn't have to wear long underwear. My legs felt so nice and slender, I didn't care if they did get cold.

I was tall, but thin. A few people asked me if I was teaching school. Alice and Helen McCabe would ask, "How tall are you Clara? You are about as tall as a tree, aren't you?"

We drove Kate, a white horse, or a team of horses to school. When it got real cold we stayed at Uncle Fred Nagel's apartment over a tavern. In the evening Uncle Fred would walk back and forth, memorizing his Masonic lecture. We girls all slept in one bed. We nailed fabric to a folding screen to have privacy when Uncle Fred or his son, Ray, walked by. The manager of the tavern downstairs asked Uncle Fred if we were cracking nuts because we were making so much noise hammering the covering on the frame. When Ray came home late and was sick, we would be scared and didn't sleep much those nights.

When we walked on the sidewalks, the city children called us hayseeds and other names. We didn't say anything, but it hurt. When it came to graduation, it was a hayseed who was valedictorian.

My second year in high school I rode Nellie or walked the four miles if Dad needed her in the field. I left her in a livery stable, the caretaker unsaddled and saddled her for me. After school I always had to wait until the train went by for Nellie to stop switching and snorting, as she was terribly afraid of it.

In the winter, I boarded with Mrs. Snitker right across from what we called Beeman (West) town. She didn't want to use too much electricity, so I had a kerosene lamp in my bedroom, but instead of studying, I read Zane Grey's books.

The third year I again rode Nellie or walked. The man at the livery stable seemed so nice and he had a little hut with a pot belly stove, where I could get my knickers off while he took care of Nellie. I stuffed my skirt into the knickers. Mother made them for us, they were like slacks, only they had a cuff just below the knee.

I stayed home a year after high school. I was only seventeen and too young to teach. Some of the days were very long, and I would look and look out of the window to see if my younger sisters were coming home from school.

Teaching

After I was through with high school I visited a pen pal I had for five years in Muscatine, Martha Freyermuth. She wanted me to come there and work in a canning factory with her, which I planned to do, until I was offered the chance to teach.

One day I was talking to a family friend, Ralph Leppert, in Waukon, and a man came and talked too. He talked so Irish, I thought he was Irish. He said, "I have a little school you can teach." I was real glad. There were so many who took "Normal Training" and the state exams, that it was very difficult to get a school to teach.

One day in July mother and I tried to find the school. When we got to this place, which seemed a long ways, there was a man plowing. We asked for directions to the school. I didn't know it was Clarence, my future husband. He told us to keep going, it would be about a mile. When I first saw the school, I felt it was in a beautiful but lonely valley.

When school started I boarded at Dewey Leppert's awhile. Andrew Leppert, Dewey's dad, died before school started. Mother and I went to the funeral, he was buried in the May's Prairie cemetery. I will always remember that a quartet sang, "We'll Never Say Good-bye in Heaven." I felt I couldn't stand it if it were my loved one who had died.

Later that year I came to stay with Clarence and his

sister Sadie, who lived next to Dewey. I got sixty-five dollars a month for teaching plus two dollars and fifty cents for starting my own fire. I felt rich when I got my first check.

The school was down the creek a mile from Clarence's home. I was eighteen. I had twelve pupils and a dog, who waited patiently every day until school was out. Attendance was very poor.

The road past the school was very little traveled. If the pupils saw a team of horses, a buggy, a wagon, or a tractor go by, they would start to scream, get out of their seats and run to the windows. It took them a long time to calm down. I don't know if they were afraid of being kidnapped, but the girl who taught the year before I did was also scared when a car or tractor went by.

When it rained I walked with the children who lived across the creek to the place where they had to cross to be sure there wasn't a flood and that they got across all right. I let school out early when it rained. Three of the families lived across the creek. They couldn't come to school if there was a flood. One of the fathers cut a tree and it was laid across the creek, but sometimes it was covered with water. At one time the flood covered the valley between the hills, and the school building was completely surrounded by water.

At noon and recess we had a lot of fun, sometimes playing baseball. Sometimes we used a butterfly net and caught suckers and fried them on an open fire and added them to our lunch.

During the school year I had a box social, and the women and girls brought pretty decorated boxes filled with goodies, and the men bought them. The usual price was two dollars, unless a boyfriend had others raising his bid on his girlfriend's box and he would pay as much as eight dollars for it. The school children gave a short program at the social and the young folks of the neighborhood put on a play. The total amount made was about thirty-two dollars. I bought a little Victrola with part of the money we made from the box social, and a little kerosene burning stove to heat soup at noon.

There was wood for me to burn in the good old pot belly stove, and a sturdy axe for me to chop kindling to get a fire started. Almost every Monday, things were a bit unsettled in the school room, cigarette stubs on the desks and mud on the floor, where hunters had had a little party. The porch door didn't have a key and was never locked. One morning I was sort of dreaming and not wondering if hunters had had a party. I opened the porch door, and my seventeen-year-old pupil, Elizabeth Sullivan, grabbed me and screamed as loud as she could. It is a wonder I didn't have a heart attack.

There were many birds. We had a book that had pictures and literature about the different birds. They became our friends. As I walked to school in the mornings, a chickadee flew from one fence post to the other, waiting for crumbs from my sandwich.

The county superintendent was W. L. Peck, who was superintendent for many years. He said, "Don't let me visit your school and find you aren't playing with the children."

Our teacher meetings were in the courthouse, which is now a museum. At one meeting the superintendent was talking about health, good food, and exercising. He showed us how much muscle he had in his arms and pointed to me to feel his big muscles. It was very embarrassing.

The next year I taught in Franklin township, eight miles

from Waukon, but I managed to get home weekends no matter how far I had to walk or how stormy it was. One weekend the snow was so deep that when my folks met me with a team of horses and sled, I fell into the sled, I was so exhausted.

Courtship

For much of the time at Clarence's, I didn't think he liked me, but one night I was on my knees petting their Airedale dog, and looked up at him. His eyes were full of love.

After the little school in French Creek township was out for the year, I went home to help my parents for the summer. In the fall I taught in a school in Franklin township. Clarence would come to see me as often as he could, but a farmer's life is a busy life.

Sometimes on Sunday nights, I wouldn't know if he could come or not. I would sit upstairs and look out the window. I would be so glad when I would see a car coming down the road.

If he came Sunday afternoon, we would sometimes drive to a neighboring town. There is always something beautiful to see. We would often just sit and talk to Mother and Dad and my sisters and whoever was visiting for the day.

Getting Married

Things were a lot different when Clarence and I were married June 12, 1929. Young couples weren't married in a church then. We were married in my parents home, who lived south of Waukon. We were married under an arch of fresh roses that my aunt Lizzie Beall lovingly created. My sister Esther was bridesmaid and Odean Sandry was best man. Reverend Ruben Elliker was the pastor, and Mrs. Elliker played the wedding march. Mother had a big angel food cake baked and a delicious meal prepared.

Clarence asked me where I would like to go on a wedding trip. I said to Pike's Peak, Colorado. It was a busy time to go on a trip as it was haying time. Ferd Buege and Otto Schburt worked at it while we were gone. We went on a bus to the top of Pike's Peak. It was so cold we had to keep passing our hands over our eyelids to keep them from freezing shut. Along the way up there were lakes and beautiful evergreens, on the top it was all ice.

We continued our driving, but I couldn't stand the high altitude and had a hemorrhage from my nose. The blood spattered the windshield. I went into a filling station restroom with my nose bleeding a lot, until I knew he wanted to close. We stopped at a farm home, where the man brought out of pail of ice water and with a dipper kept pouring the water over the length of my left arm, and it stopped the bleeding. I felt very weak.

Although there were some hard things as I grew up, there were many good things. I was glad to have six sisters and parents that loved me. And Clarence. The Lord was merciful to me.

Chickens

During 1929, the year we were married, and for a couple of years afterwards, we raised chickens by setting hens. Setting hens are hens that don't lay eggs any more. They just want to set. We moved these hens out of the chicken house into a different building. We would give them thirteen or fifteen fertile eggs. Sometimes they would set, sometimes they wouldn't. If the eggs were kept warm it would be twenty-one days before the chicks would peep out of the shells. We put each hen in a little house or box on the lawn, and would board it up at first so the little chicks could get out but not the mother hen.

Later we bought a brooder house and stove, but it still wasn't easy to raise chickens. When they were about six weeks old they would pick each other to death. We would have to catch them and dab pine tar on them.

Blocks of Ice

In the 1930s we kept our food cold with ice. The ice box was behind the door in the east wall of the kitchen. Clarence cut ice out of a pond, usually someone was with him. The blocks of ice were stored in sawdust in the ice house.

A block of ice was placed in the left corner of the ice box. It dripped down into a pan underneath. A block lasted more than a day, depending on the temperature.

We made lots and lots of homemade ice cream. We had it for every special occasion and, it seemed, every Fourth of July. There was always someone willing to turn the freezer and someone to hit the chopped ice down and to add salt. The lucky person got to lick the beater when it was taken out.

We also kept food cold with "the icy ball," which was two large balls connected by a curved rod. Every morning the unit was taken to the basement, where one ball was placed on a flame. A tub of water stood by. I don't remember if the other ball was put in that. The unit was carried to the kitchen where the cold ball was put inside the cabinet. The other ball stayed on the outside. It did a nice job of keeping the food cold, but when we heard there were kerosene burning refrigerators, we bought one.

It was nice and tall. There was a freezing unit in the center with trays of ice cubes. One tray held a double layer of ice cubes in which I made ice cream many, many times. The recipe is at the end of this article. I missed that tray long after we had electricity.

The kerosene burner was in the bottom part of the refrigerator. It didn't seem to use much kerosene. It was still working just fine when we got electricity.

Refrigerator Ice Cream
2 eggs   1 c. rich milk
1 c. cream   1 tsp. vanilla
10 tbsps. white syrup or honey, about 2/3 cup.
Some may want to use sugar.

Beat yolks, add syrup or honey. Beat until light and fluffy. Add cream, milk, and vanilla. Mix well and pour in a tray where the mixture will freeze. When firm, add to the beaten (stiff) whites. Keep on beating as you add the frozen mixture by spoonfuls. Return to the tray and freeze.

Telephones

About 1930 we had a phone on the wall, and a crank to turn when we wanted to call someone. Each of us had a number of rings. There were thirteen families on the line, six of the rings we heard, the other seven we didn't hear. We hoped we wouldn't have a long distance call because it was almost impossible to hear, for all the neighbors were listening in to find out the latest news. The operator was kind and would repeat for us. If there was a fire or something important, she would ring one long ring, then we would listen to find out what happened.

One time Bill Buege was here. It was a cold stormy winter day, but he walked ten miles to Lansing because he was thirsty. I jokingly said, "Let us know if you get there okay." To my surprise late in the afternoon the phone rang and it was our nice operator saying, "Bill Buege is at the office here and wants you to know he got to town all right."

Butchering

We would butcher a beef and two or three pigs at one time, usually someone helped. It was delicious meat all winter, but it meant a lot of work. Each time we butchered I canned about one hundred quarts of beef chunks in quart jars in a hot water bath. That meat had a delicious flavor all its own.

We used the sausage stuffer to make rings of sausage; they were put on a pole and smoked. Some years we would cure beef for dried beef. We cut the pork heads in little pieces for head cheese. We also made liver sausage. The bacon pieces and hams were put in a salt brine.

After the butchering, canning, and sausage making was done, we had the unpleasant job of rendering the lard, stirring and stirring the fat pieces in a big kettle until they were liquid. After we cooked the lard a long time, what were called cracklings would go to the top. They were brown and crisp. Some people ate those crisp cracklings, others made soap out of them.

Quilting

Up until the early Fifties we used to have quilting parties. There were seven in our group. We met in the wintertime when there weren't gardens to take care of. We all brought some food to make it easier for the lady who was having the quilting bee. We went to the quilting bee as early as we could, having our morning work done at home. We got there at different times. We felt we had to have the quilt done in one day. It gets dark early in winter months, and we were usually finished by five o'clock. Mothers with small children weren't asked to come. I suppose it was felt it would be too disturbing.

There are two kinds of quilts, quilted quilts and tied quilts. A quilted quilt was a very rare and precious thing. A quilted quilt is sewed by hand with tiny stitches going through the other side. A tied quilt is tied with yarn, putting the needle through the quilt in spaces and tying two knots. We all worked on the same quilt, although then they were regular bed size, probably seventy-two inches by ninety inches. We didn't have queen size and king size quilts at that time.

We cut designs out of cardboard for the plain fabric, tracing around them lightly with sewing chalk so it would rub off. There are many quilt patterns. Most of them are made of tiny pieces of fabric. We sometimes had embroidered blocks, which didn't have a quilted design on them. The embroidered blocks would be all finished, then probably sewed to a block of fabric the same size, then quilted, making a pretty pattern.

Most of the quilt frames were made by the sewing women's husbands. The quilt frames were made from one-by-fours. We tacked the sides of the quilt to the frames with thumb tacks.

I like the quilts with embroidered blocks, set out with a matching color. I like bright, cheerful colors. Some of the quilt patterns are Star, Tie, Basket, Nine Patch, Double Nine Patch, Wedding Ring, Grandmother's Flower Garden, Trip Around the World, Log Cabin, State.

Meals for Threshers

When the grain was ripe it was put in shocks, most people placing six bundles together and a bundle on top to keep the rain from soaking in. The grain was usually oats, sometimes it was barley, which was scratchy and made us itch. Afterwards, the dry grain was put in the huge threshing machine, which separated the kernels of grain from the straw. We expected sixteen to eighteen men when we threshed, and they worked from sunrise to sunset.

For many years Marie Fritz and I helped each other cooking meals. In the morning we would put a bench outside, and place two wash tubs of water on it, two or three basins, a couple of combs, and a mirror.

Some people gave lunch both forenoon and afternoon, the women taking it to the field. We took lunch only afternoons. We would take sandwiches, cookies or doughnuts, coffee and real homemade lemonade. Two or three days before threshing, we would bake two or three batches of cookies. Threshing day we usually had a big beef roast, mashed potatoes and gravy, two or three vegetables, cheese, and always two kinds of pie.

For supper we usually had meat balls, meat loaf, baloney or wieners, escalloped potatoes or potato salad, vegetables, cake, cookies, and sauce.

One time when Clarence was helping thresh at a neighbor's, they were served delicious clover blossom wine. It tasted like flavored sugar water, but after a little, the table began to go around; pretty soon it was going around so fast, it was hard to catch the food when it went by. After awhile, all was well again.

The next big group of men worked on silo filling, then corn shredding. As it got cold, the men got together again to saw wood. If one neighbor worked for another five days and the other one worked two days, there was never anything said about one owing the other.

Home a Hotel?

Sometimes my home seemed like a hotel.

There were two homeless men who came often and would stay sometimes two or three weeks at a time. They would finally leave to go some other place for a little while but would soon be back again.

We were looking at pictures one night, when one of the men was here. Ruth, our daughter, was a beautiful young girl. We didn't know until a long time later that Myron put one of her pictures in his pocket and told people everywhere

My parents:
Carolena Nagel and
Adolph Siekmeier.
Their wedding photo.

Anna, Lydia, me,
and Mary. We had
button shoes, too,
but I guess we had
graduated from
those.
These are laced.

Mary, Lydia, Dorothy, Esther, Anna, Ruth, me, mother and Bob.

Dorothy, Ruth, Esther, me, Lydia, Anna, Mary.

Clarence and me for our wedding photo.

Roger, Bob, and Howard.

Bob, Ruth, and Howard. Howard was always such a serious person, but you can see that something is tickling Bob.

Clarence and I had this photo taken for the county atlas in 1979.

Ruth, Howard, Clarence, Bob, and me.

he went that she was his girlfriend.

We had a lot of agents who managed to come about noon. Every time I saw one was outside talking to the men, I put another plate on the table. It was easy to have one more, and we always had a nice visit.

One time Andrew Wacker was with us at dinner time; he emptied the horseradish jar. We thought he didn't know what he had, it was like a nice mound of mashed potatoes. He enjoyed it a lot it seemed, until the last mouthful.

The telephone repairmen asked if they could eat here. I would have five or six men three days in succession for the noon meal (for several years). They would pay 75 cents a plate. I saved the money and bought a used piano that I still have. When Clarence brought it from Waukon, the hill was very steep by the May's Prairie Cemetery, and he lost the bench. He realized it had fallen out and stopped for it. When the man carried it in the house, one of them said, "This piano is so heavy, you will find it in the basement one of these days."

Sometimes fishermen would stop in the morning, and ask if they could have a noon meal. They were always nice men, they wanted to pay a dollar each.

One time a bus full of prisoners worked down at the creek making hiding places for the trout. One of two men would stop in every morning for drinking water. They were all nice looking young men and I wondered why they were prisoners at Luster Heights. I felt sorry for them and each day gave them a three pound coffee tin of homemade cookies. Later a neighbor asked, "Did you let them in the house?" I didn't have any fear about it.

A couple of years later a man and a pretty girl came to

the house. I recognized him at once as being one of the prisoners. He said, "This is my wife, I want you to meet her. I want you to know we appreciated all those cookies you gave us, and I want my wife to see where we made hiding places for the trout. Your neighbors were so good to us, they always waved when we went by. We worked near Decorah later, and they treated us just like prisoners."

I said, "Won't you tell us your name and where you live? I'd like to hear from you sometimes." He said, "We will stop on our way back from the creek." I said, "I will have lunch ready for you." The lunch waited and waited but they didn't stop.

I don't know how long three ex-soldiers stayed here when they got back from the service, Art Swenson, John Fritz and Ronnie Haas. They needed good meals, and to think of other things than war.

I had young folks stopping in for meals a lot when my sons, Howard and Bob, were teenagers. One day it was supper time and three or four extra lads came to eat. One of them said, "I caught a turtle down at the creek, you can fix it for supper." I said, "I don't know how to cook a turtle." He said, "I'll tell you." I ate a little bit, just so I could say I'd eaten turtle.

If we weren't gone, we almost always had a group of people for Sunday dinner.

A German came to the neighborhood, we felt he had escaped prison. He was almost always angry. He would be here a month or more at a time, cutting wood. After he got up in the morning he would walk around the house five or six times screaming. I asked him what was the matter; he said in German, "God in Heaven, the devil for us all. I tell the whole world."

When he would be in the woods working, all of the neighbors could hear his sermons. I didn't feel it was safe to have him in the house, but Clarence felt it was all right, and we needed a lot of wood.

Wolves

There were many wolves in the 1930s. We heard them often in the night. Two or three could make so much noise howling, we wouldn't know whether or not it was a pack of wolves.

One day Clarence was plowing with a team of horses. A wolf followed all day about the length of a car behind him. He felt sure there were baby wolves close by, so he and a neighbor looked in the woods as it was getting dark. They found five baby wolves in a hollow tree. I feel sure they were cute, but the wolves were killing baby calves, so they felt forced to kill them. Clarence said the wolf clawed at the tree and howled the whole night.

Our Delco Plant

We had a Delco plant in the 1930s, which used a wind charger or motor to charge the batteries. There was a wire from the charger or motor to the batteries. The motor had to run when I used the Maytag wash machine or when I ironed. I had big washes and in those days we did a lot of ironing too. I was always glad to finish so the motor could be shut off. I didn't like the noise, it made me nervous.

Every time we had company, Howard and Bob, our sons, would climb almost to the top of the wind charger. It would sway back and forth. They weren't scared but their mother was. I would say to the company, "Don't look at them and maybe they will come down."

There were twenty-two batteries on shelves in the basement. Our electrician, Max Daniels, came often to check on them and he enjoyed having supper with us. He never married. He liked to hold Ruth, who was small, and would talk and talk to her.

One evening he was checking the batteries. As I was getting supper, I heard a terrible bang. I wondered if our electrician was dead or alive. I opened the basement door just in time to hear a blast of swear words, so I knew he was alive. I don't know what he had done to blow things up but his hands were burned. He rubbed black grease on them. It must have helped because he stayed to eat supper with us.

Hair

Hair styles used to be quite different. For a quick curl we had curling irons that we heated in a kerosene lamp. The curling iron was something like a scissors. We grabbed our hair and rolled it after the curling iron was warm, not hot. If we went to a beauty shop we could get a marcel, which was the name of a hair style. The instrument that made it was also called a marcel and was something like a double curling iron.

We also had curved combs. If we fastened them just right in our hair, we would have some waves. We got one of our hair styles by teasing our hair at the ears, until we had a nice round bunch. They were called "cootie garages."

When we first had permanents, the curlers were plugged into a big wheel that hung from the ceiling. The operator had to be careful not to turn the electricity too high. I was told there was a good beauty shop in Decorah, so I went there for a permanent. The girl had the curlers too hot and burned the back of my head. It hurt for weeks, but I was too timid to report it to the shop owner. A lady in Lansing had her head burned by a permanent, all of her hair fell out and not any of it grew back.

Doctors and Nurses

Doctors and nurses didn't have it easy in the 1930s and later. For years Dr. Frederickson and Dr. Thornton were in Lansing. Both of them made many, many house calls both day and night. If one of their patients was seriously sick, they would sit by their bedside all night long. Of all the many times we saw them, neither was ever cross.

When we went to see Dr. Thornton, Mrs. Thornton always came to the waiting room and said, "You can see Dr. Thornton pretty soon." She always had great big bedroom slippers on. Sometimes she would call him about some difficulty, and you had to wait until he came back.

She tried to protect him from being too busy and would sometimes take the receiver off the hook. When we would tell her we tried to call for several hours, she would say, "Oh! I am sorry the grandchildren were here and took the receiver off the hook."

When someone was sick or a new baby was expected, you could have a nurse in your home for a reasonable price. We had a nurse in our home when Roger and Bob were born. We had such a lovely nurse when Roger was born.

Bob was born with baby jaundice, and had a lot of phlegm in his throat. The nurse stood by his crib for hours, watching so he wouldn't choke. She fixed my toast for breakfast before she went to bed at night so she wouldn't have to get up early. I was thankful I didn't break my teeth on the hard toast.

Clarence and I Loved Horses

Clarence loved his big faithful draft horses. We always had six. Every morning before they were hitched up to go to work, they were tenderly brushed and curried, and again at the end of the day when they were through working. Sometimes one of the horses wouldn't like the hired man and would kick him, and Clarence would have to harness it.

One summer we needed another horse so Clarence bought one. She would be in the field working and would suddenly lay down. Clarence would think she was sick and take her harness off, and she would jump up as well as could be, and try to run off. Clarence and the boys, Howard and Bob, didn't like a tricky horse and she was soon sold.

The men were very careful to rest the horses during the

hot days. We never lost a horse in the heat. They weren't given water when they were real hot.

There was a lot of sleeping sickness in the horses one summer. Our big, good, faithful Bob got it. The vet, Dr. Saewert helped fix a frame, holding him high up off his feet. He stayed in the frame about a month. The men tenderly kept ice packs on his head to help the fever. He got pretty good again, but had to think a little when given orders to go or stop. Dr. Saewert was a caring vet. The vet before that would say, "I think it needs some whiskey." Then he would say, "I have to see if it is all right," and drink too much of it.

Clarence shipped cattle to Chicago many times, and would go along on the train to see that they were fed properly and given water. One time while he was in Chicago a beautiful American saddle horse was brought from a southern state. Clarence felt she would be a good horse for the boys. A man who had just brought turkeys to Chicago brought Blondie here in his pickup. She was a wild, spirited horse. Clarence felt that if I rode her all winter she would be tame for the boys in the spring. We didn't know then that a spirited horse shouldn't be ridden in winter weather. I had done a lot of riding before I was married, but I was scared of her. Each time before I rode her, I sat in a chair and said the 121st Psalm. Someone would hold her so I could get in the saddle. We only had a poor, small saddle then, an army saddle. One day as I rode past John Weber's farm (next to ours), they started up a tractor to grind feed. Away went Blondie. There was so much snow the ditch was filled with it. She jumped into the ditch and fell. I was thrown quite a ways ahead of her. I ran back and caught her bridle before she could run away. John held her so I could get in the saddle again. I felt pretty sore and stiff for several days. I didn't want the boys to be afraid of her and know that I had been thrown, so I tried to walk nice and straight. She made such a fuss that I didn't try to make her go past Webers again. We would go down to the creek.

We raised two colts, Blondie II and Beauty sired by Alden Larson's stallion that was beautiful, also wild and spirited. Ruth, my daughter, and I rode them on trail rides, but Clarence always worried there wouldn't be a good loading place and they would have a leg broken. We were charter members of the Saddle Club, and I still go to their suppers sometimes.

Clarence and I went to many horse shows and liked the ones at the Waterloo Dairy Congress. We liked the horse shows at West Salem, Wisconsin, too, but we didn't enjoy them so much when walking through the stables. We saw horses that didn't win a prize being punished.

Both Blondie and Beauty were beautiful American saddle horses, but Clarence felt Beauty was special and should be gaited and trained to be a show horse. She was in a training place near Waterloo for two summers. We went to see her one day unexpectedly, and one of the men hired to help take care of the horses was whipping her. We felt awful. Clarence told the manager he would come the next day with the truck to get her. When they got there the next day, they couldn't find something they needed to load her. She knew the truck and jumped in while they were hunting.

We sold Blondie I to Vince Strub. He had a hard time with her, she didn't want him to saddle her. He felt she was the fastest horse he had ever seen. They timed her with a car. She could run thirty-five or forty miles an hour. He said, "I won't believe it that Clara Leppert rode her," but I did.

Ruth and I rode Blondie and Beauty in parades sometimes. They were well matched. Clarence was so proud of them, but they were so scared of all of the noise. They were like unbroken colts every spring. We worried to watch Howard try to tame them. He had a bad back and sometimes they tried to throw him. Clarence and the boys felt they should be sold before someone was hurt. We sold them to friends, Nick and Margurite DeLair of Jamestown, North Dakota. They paid seventy-five dollars each, which was too cheap, but horses weren't selling high then. They kept them a long time and raised several colts. Ruth and I cried as Clarence left with them in the truck.

We Walked in a Circle

The Walsh's were neighbors who lived south of us. About two weeks after World War II started, their daughter Dorothy's husband was killed in action.

Ruth and I were going to walk there to try and express our sympathy to the family. We thought we wouldn't get lost if we followed a fence, but soon there was a huge ditch we had to walk around. If we could have walked straight, it probably would have been a mile, but we had to go around too many ditches.

After some time we saw a house. It was hard to believe it was Orness's house. We had walked a circle in tall weeds. We were full of burrs and tired. We thought we would visit Rose awhile. She said, "Here is a pan, you can pick those burrs off." By the time we had the pan almost full of burrs it was time to go home.

We sent a sympathy card and letter to Walsh's instead of trying to walk there again.

The Methodist Church on the Hill

The little Methodist church on the hill in Lansing township was incorporated in 1858. Clarence's father, Phillip Leppert, was one of the pioneers who helped hew out the stone for the church.

The church was in good shape until about the late Thirties. Andrew Hirth paid the money for a new roof. At times there were services. Sometimes an evangelist would come and there would be a series of meetings at night. Clarence and I went to one of the meetings. The evangelist was walking up to the church as we were. He said, "Tonight my sermon will be on the devil's stick." We didn't know what that was but found out it was the cigar.

The women of the area would meet with the people of the Evangelical Church in Lansing and hold Ladies Aid meetings in our home. The lunch was more like a supper. We often made homemade ice cream. We paid ten cents a month dues.

I think Reverend Prust was the pastor. He called at the homes asking for a little money toward his salary. Some gave him money, others gave him meat, chickens, or eggs. Some gave him oats for his horse. The parsonage was west of the church.

The last time I was in the little Methodist church was probably in 1939. My daughter Ruth was a baby. It was

Sophia Frahm's funeral, the church was full. Someone held Ruth while I climbed the ladder to the tiny balcony. The doves flew back and forth cooing, while the minister spoke. Sophia had loved flowers and birds. The doves were trying to say they loved her.

We marvel that the steeple still stays on the church. It is tilted on the southeast corner. Carol Dee said the Lord is holding it up.

Chivari

A long time ago when a couple was married the neighbors would get together and chivari them. We would pound on circle saws, dish pans, and whatever else would make a big racket. The couple would finally come out of the house and invite us in for a party or give us money to have a party later.

Sometimes the new bride wasn't in favor of the noise and wouldn't come out of the house, and the bridegroom would invite the visitors in for whatever was convenient for lunch, and the men would enjoy themselves.

When Booty Hirth and Abbie Pfiffner were married, we again went with equipment to make noise. We were sorry to learn later that fifty chickens, about six weeks old, crowded in a corner and smothered to death. They couldn't stand the noise. The smiling, happy couple came outside to greet us, and to give our leader some money for a party to be held later.

One time we chivaried a couple in Lansing. It may have been against the city ordinance, but the new couple was a jolly pair, who didn't let the racket last long by coming outside with a gift of money. The Lansing officers were kind and didn't say anything. It was the last chivari party, I was told.

Thanksgiving Days

We had many good Thanksgiving days of which we think often. One time the weather changed our big plans. I had a huge turkey and invited all of my relatives in and near Waukon to come. It wasn't going to be potluck, I was going to prepare all of the food.

I prepared all the food that I could on Wednesday. It rained that night and froze. When we got up Thursday morning, everything was all ice. As we expected, I had to phone that it was too dangerous to try to come. My first thought was, What would I do with all of the food? No one would want to drive very far on the treacherous roads. I wondered if Earl Gruber and his family had plans. They lived two farms down the road. I talked to Clarence, and we invited them to come for dinner. They drove to our place safely. We were glad to have some one share our food, but there was a lot left for other days.

One Thanksgiving we took care of two turkeys, one was for the Saddle Club. We were charter members. For the first time Clarence said it was better to stick their necks instead of cutting off their heads. He tied them to the clothesline that went across the basement. After they were dead, we picked them. The wing feathers were very difficult to pull so we each took a pliers to pull them out. We were finally finished, and let the first turkey down and laid it on the table. When Clarence took the second turkey down, away ran the naked bird, jumping and flying over everything in the basement, with both of us after it. We would almost catch it, but it would fly again. It took us quite a while to catch it. Clarence never suggested sticking a turkey again.

Hunting Coon Was Fun

Men still go hunting coon, and maybe women too, but I don't think they have as much fun as Clarence did. As he worked during the day, he thought how much fun it would be to get a coon that night. Howard or Bob, or both, or a neighbor, would go with him. They usually had a lunch, which was a sandwich or oyster stew before they left, and they dressed up warm.

We never had a real hunting dog, but our plain mutt dogs were good hunters. Sometimes a big forty pound coon wouldn't die right away as expected after being shot, and would drop out of the tree, very angry, to fight with the poor dog.

One night they saw a dog, and when they got closer, found it was guarding its master's jacket. We never knew how long the hunter had left his dog, waiting for him to return. Another night a friendly black dog followed Bob and Howard home. We couldn't find out who its owner was, and felt he was going to stay with us, but one day he disappeared.

We felt his owner saw him as he drove by, and put him in his car.

I was always glad when I knew the coon hunters were home. They would drink hot milk or coffee and have toast with butter and jam. It helped warm them up, but I don't think it did much for their cold feet. They didn't care that they didn't have much sleep, they had had a good time.

One lovely, sunny day there was a knock at the door. It was Rose Orness, a neighbor, who had walked here. She said, "I have a coon in salt water, we are having it for supper tonight, come and eat with us." We had never had coon, but we were willing to try it. We were surprised that it was good. She showed the recipe to us. It was long. She said she had to put all of those ingredients in the dressing to make it taste good.

We had a friend who had a pet coon for a long time, it was beautiful. Every time we saw Merrill, the coon was with him. He rode in the front seat of the car like a dog. Merrill never married, so the coon was good company for him. It had its chair at the table every time he ate his meals. One evening Merrill was very tired from working hard all day, and went to the chicken house to feed his precious chickens before dark. He felt, "I can't cry, I'm a grown man," as he looked in horror at twelve dead chickens on the floor and a naughty coon in the corner. That was the end of the coon he had had a long time and had learned to love.

Ole and Rose Were Good Neighbors

Rose Rothermel was married to Jack May. They had one child, Harold. Jack died suddenly. Harold loved working in the woods, and Rose felt she needed help on the farm.

When Dewey Leppert's father went to North Dakota to look after the land he had there, Rose told him that if he met a nice man there, to bring him along home with him. He brought Ole Orness, who was a good and honest person. He was born in Norway and spoke often of his life there, before he came to America. He worked as a hired man at first, but gradually they began to love each other and were married.

One of the first things Ole wanted were pure bred Ayrshire cattle like they had in Norway. He gave each cow and calf a name. I often took pictures of them for him. Ole loved animals. He had a tiny spotted terrier that he patiently taught many tricks. I thought the cutest was when she stood on her hind legs, put her front paws on a chair, and bowed her head to pray. Ole would look at her with loving eyes, he was so proud of her.

Rose was a good cook. She said many times, "Butter makes good things better." Her specialty was sponge cake, which she made often. Her homemade bread was delicious. When she finally had an electric stove, she would fix one egg at a time in a huge frying pan, no matter how many eggs she fixed, so grease wouldn't spatter on her precious stove. She was a careful housekeeper, too. If you had a little mud on your shoes, you left them on the porch until you went home.

She had a squeaky violin. Sometimes when we went there evenings, she would play polkas and waltzes. Ole was so proud of her. As Rose grew older, she felt she was allergic to the lilacs around their home, so Ole had to dig them out. I missed them, it seemed their place looked bare.

Harold, her son, died suddenly, doing the work he loved, cutting trees. I don't think he knew it, but it was found that his heart was on his right side. His wife also died and Ole and Rose lovingly took his four children, Louise, Betty, Adeline, and Carl, into their home. They went to school near French Creek. Carl is married and lives in Waukon. I don't know where the girls are now. Adeline was a tiny baby when born, weighing less that four pounds and fit nicely in a shoe box.

Rose went to town many times with a team of horses and wagon or sled to get feed ground. She always came home about nine o'clock p.m. At that time we had to go almost two miles for our mail. She would stop at the first neighbor's with their mail, and they would call the next neighbor saying, "Go up to the road, Rose is coming with the mail." I have a shelf unit in my kitchen porch yet. One shelf was for Dewey and Florence Leppert's mail, the other shelf for Ole and Rose's mail.

When Dewey Leppert felt he needed a new car, he bought a very nice one. Once when the road had snow drifts, he left it in Ole's yard and walked home from there. Ole kept his precious sheep in the yard at night, so stray dogs wouldn't attack and kill them. In a few days the wind went down, the snow plow cleared the road and Dewey went to get his nice new car. He was shocked and a little angry to see both doors on one side crushed in. The sheep buck had gone to see what that new thing in the yard was. He saw his reflection in it and thought he had a rival, so he bunted the doors in with his tough head.

One morning I thought I heard a funny noise. I looked out of the east window to see Ole's car in the ditch. He was on his way to a soil conservation meeting. He helped measure land without pay, and urged his neighbors to do contour and strip farming. He must have forgotten for a second that he was driving a car as he leaned out of the window to blow out his nose. Willard Leppert was with him. Willard's window was open, and they were in a bed of elderberries, and Willard's face was splashed with elderberry juice. Willard said afterward that Ole thought it was blood. He looked so worried and asked Willard, "Willard are you hurt?"

Ole and Rose tried to economize, and didn't have a phone. Ole came here many, many times to have me make phone calls for him, as he didn't hear well. One morning he came, looking very sad. He said, "Will you please call the filling station in Lansing and tell them to call the man who picks up dead animals to come for my sheep." I don't know who answered, but he thought I said, "Tell the man Ole Orness is dead." A couple days later Ole went to the grocery store to buy his groceries. It was filled with people doing their shopping. They all looked at Ole like they had seen a ghost. Before Ole could ask why they were staring at him a lady said, "We thought you were dead." Mr. and Mrs. Pat Welch were good friends of Ole, so that day they went to Lansing for Ole's wake. Mr. Saam had a little room off his furniture store where he placed the casket. As the Welches were getting out of their car, someone said, "Hello." They turned to see Ole walking by. They almost fell over in shock.

Ole was going with others to another soil conservation meeting. The car was in the yard, so he hurriedly kissed Rose and went to the waiting car. He was seated but said to the driver, "Please wait a minute." He went to the house and kissed Rose again. When they were near Luana, the car went down a terrible, steep embankment. Ole didn't realize he was hurt badly and helped lift Mr. Marti's body into an ambulance. Ole was in a hospital a long time with a broken pelvis bone. When Rose was told Ole had been in a car accident, she said, "I'm not shocked, he never kissed me twice before when he left on a trip."

In Ole's later years, he developed bladder and prostrate trouble and had to have surgery. He didn't have any health insurance. The doctor asked him if there was someone who could take care of him. He said, "Rose isn't well enough, but maybe Clara Leppert would take care of me." I had never thought of being a nurse for a neighbor. The doctor gave me lots of instructions and instead of being in the hospital for a week, he was in our home a week. He was always a good neighbor, I was glad to do what I could for him. As Rose grew older, she tired easily, and asked me if I would wash her four blue dresses that were all alike. I had long instructions on how to wash them by hand and iron them. Our valley seemed warm and sheltered with Ole and Rose living here.

One morning when Howard and Bob went to check on Ole and Rose, Ole was in the house slumped in a chair with a lot of pain. He had fallen on the ice on the porch and had a broken hip. They had an old school bell that they rang when they needed help, but the wind wasn't right for us to hear it this time. After Ole came back from the hospital in Iowa City, he was taken to the home of Chet Barr, Sr., where Mrs. Barr gave him loving care. I took dinner to Rose, giving her enough food for her supper too, but she became too weak to stay alone and both she and Ole were taken to a nursing home in Cresco. We were awfully sorry that they were taken so far away.

Ole's birthday was in March, so Clarence and I took a decorated cake to him. We looked out of the window, and there was a real snow storm. Ole said he would like for us to stay longer, but he was worried about us driving home in the storm. He was always thinking of others. He told us that with the small amount of money he was given every month, he had bought a stone at the Lansing cemetery for Rose and him. Rose didn't live long. Ole lived about four years after Rose died. After he was in Cresco awhile, he was taken to West Union, where it was so far away it was difficult to see him. Clarence and I were probably about the only ones who did go.

Dixie Was a Good, Faithful Dog

Our daughter, Ruth, married Andy Beyer. We kept their little dog, Ginger, for four years while they were in Beirut, Lebanon. Andy is an engineer. When they came home to Houston, Texas, and took Ginger, Clarence felt very lonely and I felt we should get another dog.

I was on my way to Lansing one day when I heard an ad on the car radio: "Spitz dogs free." A couple of days later I drove south of Waukon to see the puppies. Only one puppy was left, she was white, tan and brown. She was nursing her mother, a pure bred white Spitz. The father was a terrier. I felt she was cute. Five inches of Dixie's tail were white.

I asked Irene what I should pay her. She said, "I don't want you to pay anything, please take me out for coffee some time." She didn't drive. It was in the fall, I was busy freezing the food from the garden. I felt so busy I sent her a check instead of taking her out for coffee. She and her son were killed in a car accident a couple of years ago. It is my regret that I didn't forget about being so busy, and did not give her a nice afternoon out to lunch.

I don't remember Dixie playing with dog toys like most puppies. When I let her outside in the morning she would hunt mice and sometimes not come back for an hour. She sat on Clarence's lap most of the time for two years, and he would talk soothingly to her. After Clarence had a stroke, it seemed she was too heavy, and he didn't want to hold her anymore. She would lay behind him as he sat in his favorite chair, and growl when anyone came near him. At night she would sleep at the foot of his bed. He developed pneumonia, and we took him to the Lutheran hospital in LaCrosse. Dixie missed him so much she chewed his bedroom slippers to tiny bits before he came back.

We took care of Clarence for three years, as he continued to have strokes. We had a hospital bed so he would be comfortable at night. Howard and Bob were wonderful, lovingly getting him out of bed mornings and wheeling him to the chair he loved, in the wheel chair. Ruth did all the things she could the times she came to visit. Barbara, Bob's wife, and Della, Howard's wife, were also dear, helping in many ways which I will always remember. The grandchildren also helped lovingly.

Dixie would always watch every night as Howard and

Bob put Clarence to bed. She didn't want anyone to touch his blankets. They couldn't resist teasing her sometimes, and she would growl at them.

Dixie seemed to realize when we took Clarence to the hospital for the last time. Lesa, Josey, and Audrey, Bob's daughters, tried to hold her but she pushed the screen door open and followed us to Howard and Della's, where their dogs chased her back home.

She was a lonely dog for a long time. She slept on a big rug in my bedroom and became my watch dog. If any one came in the house at night, she stood at the top of the stairs alerting me that someone had come.

One evening an insurance agent came at 9:30 p.m. I told him I didn't like agents to come in the late evening. She didn't like him and stood by me growling at him. When he finally left, I tried to keep her in the porch, but she pushed the screen door open and chased him all the way to his car. He was very angry and growled at me to call my dog back.

She continued to be my watch dog until she couldn't hear well anymore. I will always think of Dixie as a wonderful little dog, there will never be another dog like her. She was seventeen or eighteen years old when she died.

Closing Thoughts

This is the closing of my book. I had never thought I would be writing stories for a book. I want to thank Robert Wolf for his kindness and patience as he watched for my mistakes. I hope I haven't hurt anyone in any way, but as you read of the "simple times" of the past, may there be some small thing that will help you in some way. All of us have had some hard things in life, but we try to think of all of the joy we have had.

I thank the Lord for my loving family, Bob and Barbara, Ruth and Andy and Della, my ten grandchildren and their husbands and wives, and my ten little great-grandchildren, and all of my dear relatives and friends.

May the Lord give all of you many "special" blessings and to all who read this book.

Thank you. With love, Clara.

FREE RIVER PRESS
Folk Literature Series

Ancient Chinese emperors maintained a Music Bureau, whose function was to collect folk songs from across the empire. By these songs the emperor sought to know whether a local government functioned well, whether a duke or prince performed his duties, and whatever else might be on the people's minds.

The Free River Press folk literature series is a modest imitation of the Music Bureau. Its writings are mostly generated in Free River Press writing workshops. To date the press has worked with the homeless and with farmers, but eventually will work with Americans of all social standings and a diversity of occupations. The press hopes that thirty years hence the folk literature series will resemble a collective autobiography of America.

Free River Press Folk Literature Series:

Robert Wolf, ed. **Passing Thru.** $4.95
El Gilbert. **Lion's Share.** $4.95
Josef Goller. **From within Walls.** $4.95
Diana Schooler. **Lemme Tell You where I Used to Live.** $4.95
Rebel Yell. **Hitchhiker's Dream.** $4.95
Robert Wolf, ed. **Voices from the Land.** $5.95
Clara Leppert. **Simple Times.** $5.95

Free River Press
RR 2, Box 96
Lansing, IA 52151